T0004879

WHAT IF I NEED STITCHES?

 Gareth Stevens
PUBLISHING

BY THERESE SHEA

Please visit our website, www.garethstevens.com. For a free color catalog of all our high-quality books, call toll free 1-800-542-2595 or fax 1-877-542-2596.

Library of Congress Cataloging-in-Publication Data

Names: Shea, Therese, author.
Title: What if I need stitches? / Therese M. Shea.
Description: New York : Gareth Stevens Publishing, [2016]. | Series: Benched:
 dealing with sports injuries | Includes bibliographical references and
 index.
Identifiers: LCCN 2016012442 | ISBN 9781482448962 (pbk.) | ISBN 9781482448900 (library bound) |
ISBN 9781482448481 (6 pack)
Subjects: LCSH: Wounds and injuries–Treatment–Juvenile literature. |
 Sutures–Juvenile literature. | Sports injuries–Juvenile literature.
Classification: LCC RD73.S8 S54 2016 | DDC 617.044–dc23
LC record available at https://lccn.loc.gov/2016012442

First Edition

Published in 2017 by
Gareth Stevens Publishing
111 East 14th Street, Suite 349
New York, NY 10003

Copyright © 2017 Gareth Stevens Publishing

Designer: Katelyn E. Reynolds
Editor: Ryan Nagelhout

Photo credits: Cover, p. 1 (background photo) Alison Hancock/Shutterstock.com; cover, p. 1 (girl) sunabesyou/Shutterstock.com; cover, pp. 1–24 (background texture) mexrix/Shutterstock.com; cover, pp. 1–24 (chalk elements) Aleks Melnik/Shutterstock.com; p. 5 Laszlo66/Shutterstock.com; p. 7 Yilmaz Uslu/Shutterstock.com; p. 9 Mark Winfrey/Shutterstock.com; p. 11 Werneuchen/Wikipedia.org; p. 13 manzrussali/Shutterstock.com; p. 15 Dmitri Ma/Shutterstock.com; p. 17 Praisaeng/Shutterstock.com; p. 19 (main) Jodi Jacobson/Getty Images; p. 19 (inset) Brian Chase/Shutterstock.com; p. 21 Gregory Shamus/Getty Images.

Printed in the United States of America

CPSIA compliance information: Batch #CS16GS : For further information contact Gareth Stevens, New York, New York at 1-800-542-2595.

CONTENTS

Blood!...4

Superskin 6

How to Tell?...8

Stitched with Sutures...............................10

Getting Stitched Up 12

Caring for Stitches 14

Where'd They Go? 16

Not Quite Stitches.....................................18

Drew Miller's Stitches Story.................20

Glossary...22

For More Information 23

Index...24

 Words in the glossary appear in **bold** type the first time they are used in the text.

BLOOD!

OUCH! Getting bumped and pushed is a part of most sports—and not just in the pros. That's why many players wear pads and helmets to protect, or guard, their body. But there are still many ways to get **injured**—and that can mean blood.

Injuries can result in an open wound in the skin. Though some injuries can be small and heal easily, such as paper cuts, some wounds are more serious. They may need stitches to close them and help the skin heal.

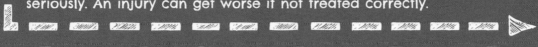

While injuries are a part of sports, it's a smart idea to take any injury seriously. An injury can get worse if not treated correctly.

Sports are just one of the ways people can get hurt enough to need stitches. Injuries happen every day, even at home.

SUPERSKIN

Not every wound needs stitches. The body works quickly to start healing when the skin is hurt. It slows the amount of blood rushing to the wound. Parts of the blood form a covering called a scab over the wound. New skin grows under the scab. The scab falls off when the skin underneath is ready.

Some wounds are very deep, wide, or serious, though. That's where stitches are needed. Stitches connect the sides of the wound so it heals well.

✖ THE GAME PLAN

1 Scabs may seem gross, but they're just dried blood. Never pick a scab. Let it fall off on its own, so it can protect the wound underneath for as long as possible.

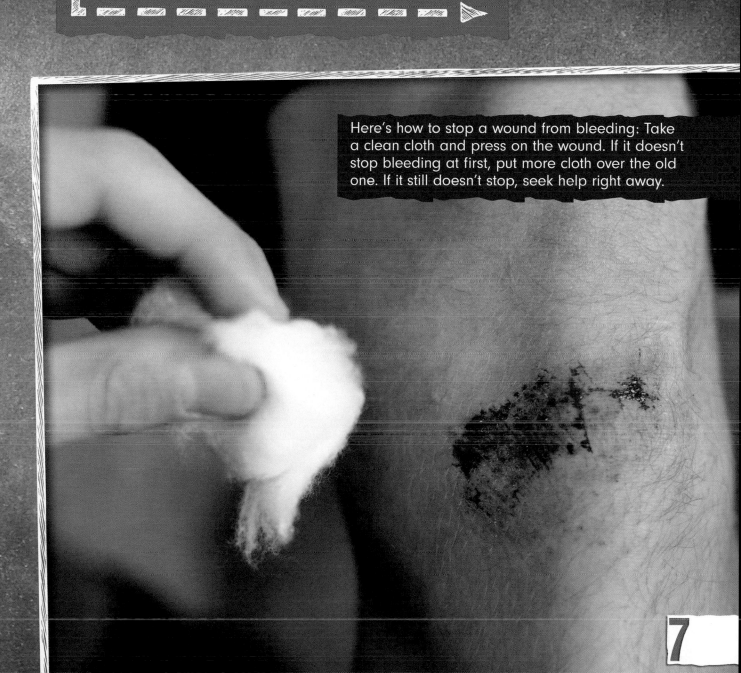

Here's how to stop a wound from bleeding: Take a clean cloth and press on the wound. If it doesn't stop bleeding at first, put more cloth over the old one. If it still doesn't stop, seek help right away.

HOW TO TELL?

How do you know if a wound needs stitches? It's not always easy to tell. However, wounds that look deep and gaping, or split apart, often need stitches. Cuts that don't stop bleeding after several minutes may need stitches, too. Any wound that looks like it won't close on its own requires **medical** attention.

Even smaller cuts in certain areas of the body may need stitches. For example, cuts to the face and especially lips need to heal perfectly so that a **scar** isn't left behind.

✖THE GAME PLAN

1 Elevate, or raise, an injury above the heart if you can. This stops the wound from swelling.

If you think you might need stitches, ask an adult to take you to an **emergency** room or other medical center.

EMERGENCY

CLEARANCE 12'

Emergency

9

STITCHED WITH SUTURES

Stitches use a kind of thread, but it's not the type used to sew clothes. It's a special thread called suture. It can be made from man-made materials, such as nylon, or natural materials, such as silk.

A suture thread has certain features. It needs to be thin enough not to leave a scar, but strong enough to hold the wound closed. It also needs to **stretch**, especially for body parts that move a lot.

✘ THE GAME PLAN

1. One natural kind of suture is made from the insides of a sheep or cow. It's called catgut!

Most sutures come with the needle already attached.
A needle holder is used to do the stitching.

GETTING STITCHED UP

Before the stitching starts, a doctor or nurse **numbs** the skin near the cut by applying a **gel** or **injecting** it with a liquid. Next, they remove dirt and anything else that may be in the wound with water and soap.

Finally, it's time to sew up the cut. For each stitch, they loop the suture through either side of the cut and tie a knot to hold the wound shut. They repeat this until the wound is totally closed.

✖ THE GAME PLAN

1 The gel and injected liquid are anesthetics (a-nuhs-THEH-tihks). These are drugs that cause a body part to lose feeling—including the feeling of pain!

You might feel tugging as the stitches come together. Don't worry, though, the skin is numb so it won't hurt.

CARING FOR STITCHES

Getting stitches is just the start, though. The doctor or nurse will give directions about how to care for the stitches. For example, stitches shouldn't get wet for the first few days. They may need a **bandage** over them for a while, too.

If there are any unusual changes to the stitches, such as swelling or oozing liquid, the wound may be **infected**. An antibiotic may be needed. An antibiotic is a drug used to kill harmful bacteria and to cure infections.

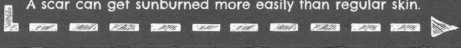

Stitches and new scars should be kept out of direct sunlight. A scar can get sunburned more easily than regular skin.

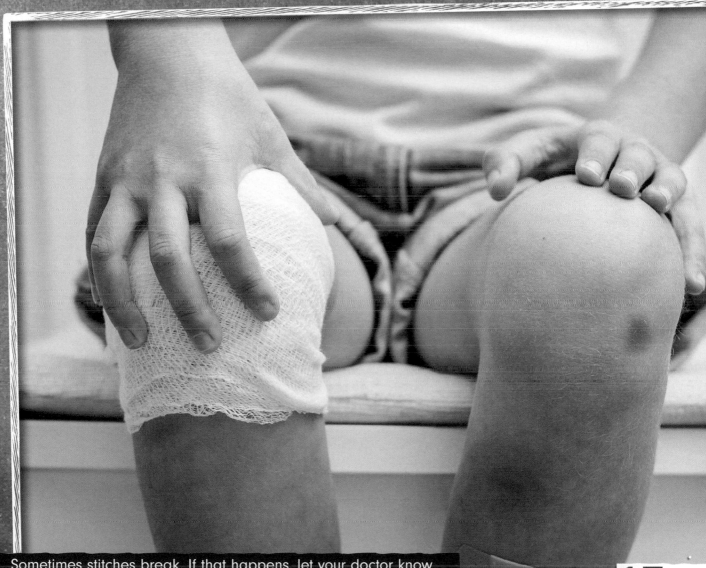

Sometimes stitches break. If that happens, let your doctor know right away. There's a chance of infection or the wound reopening.

WHERE'D THEY GO?

What happens to the sutures after the skin is healed? Some need to be taken out, usually 3 to 14 days later. Stitches on the face are removed earlier, so they don't leave scars. Stitches on other parts of the body may be removed later if the wound is more likely to reopen. When removing stitches, the doctor snips the suture near each knot and pulls the stitch out. It doesn't even hurt!

Sometimes, you don't need the stitches removed at all. They dissolve! This means that over time, they're broken down by the skin.

✖ THE GAME PLAN

Sometimes tape is placed over the injury after stitches are removed so the wound can continue to heal without suture marks.

WHAT TO EXPECT

Seek medical help for a deep, gaping, or continually bleeding wound.

An anesthetic is used to numb the skin around the wound.

The wound is cleaned.

The wound is kept dry and clean, and treated with antibiotics.

The wound is stitched up with sutures.

The sutures are removed or dissolve after about 3 to 14 days.

Remaining scars slowly flatten and lighten in color.

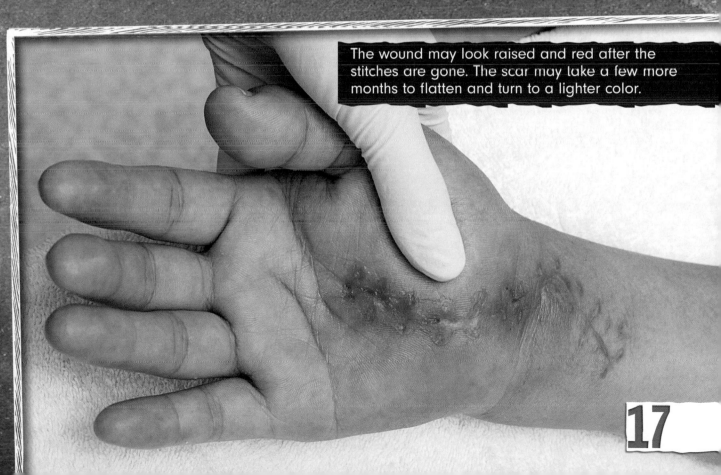

The wound may look raised and red after the stitches are gone. The scar may take a few more months to flatten and turn to a lighter color.

NOT QUITE STITCHES

Smaller cuts may not need stitches. They can be kept closed by little strips called butterfly bandages. There's also a glue that can keep a cut closed while it heals. It's good for an area where the cut is less likely to be stretched and reopened, such as the forehead.

Sometimes, a wound is held closed by special **staples**! Staples are used on longer cuts. They're faster to place than stitches. However, staples aren't used on the face as they cause more scarring than stitches.

1 Butterfly bandages come off in the bath or shower after a few days. Glue dissolves after about a week. Staples are made of metal, however, and need to removed.

Whether cuts are closed with staples, butterfly bandages, glue, or stitches depends on their location and depth.

DREW MILLER'S STITCHES STORY

Hockey players wear helmets and pads to keep safe, but injuries still happen. Detroit Red Wing Drew Miller experienced a terrible injury March 31, 2015. During a game against the Ottawa Senators, a player fell, cutting Miller's face with a knife-sharp skate.

"My first reaction was get to the doctors, the people who can help me," Miller said. He ran off the ice and received 60 stitches. Miller knows he was lucky his injury wasn't worse. His fast response helped him mend quickly. He was back on the ice 2 days later!

✖THE GAME PLAN

1. Drew Miller holds the Detroit Red Wings record for most regular season consecutive, or back-to-back, games played.

Even the **visor** Drew Miller wore couldn't guard him from his injury. Luckily, his eye wasn't affected, and his face healed with little scarring.

GLOSSARY

bandage: a strip used to cover a wound

emergency: an unexpected situation that needs quick action

gel: a thick matter like jelly

infected: having an illness because harmful organisms have entered the body

inject: to force a drug into part of the body using a needle

injured: harmed

medical: having to do with care given by doctors and nurses

numb: to cause to lose feeling

scar: a mark left by the healing of injured skin

staple: a usually metal fastener used to hold layers of something together

stretch: to become longer or wider when pulled

visor: a front part of a helmet that a player can see through, which is worn to protect the face or eyes

FOR MORE INFORMATION

BOOKS

Basen, Ryan. *Injuries in Sports*. Minneapolis, MN: ABDO Publishing Company, 2014.

Herrington, Lisa M. *I Need Stitches*. New York, NY: Children's Press, 2015.

WEBSITES

Body Science: About Stitches
pamf.org/preteen/mybody/bodyscience/pt/stitches.html
Read more about stitches on this site.

How Stitches Help Kids Heal
kidshealth.org/kid/ill_injure/aches/stitches.html
Find out all you need to know about stitches.

Stitches
pediatriconcall.com/kidscorner/whywhat/Stitches.aspx
Your questions about stitches and other health matters are answered here.

INDEX

anesthetics 13, 17

antibiotic 14, 17

bandage 14

butterfly bandages 18, 19

catgut 11

cleaning 12, 14

doctor 12, 14, 15, 16, 20

face 8, 16, 18, 20, 21

glue 18, 19

infection 14, 15

knot 12, 16

Miller, Drew 20, 21

needle 11

needle holder 11

numbing 12, 14

nurse 12, 14

open wound 4, 6, 8, 10, 12, 16, 17

scab 6, 7

scar 8, 10, 15, 16, 17, 18, 21

skin 4, 6, 12, 13, 16

staples 18, 19

suture 10, 11, 12, 16, 17